THE JIG

Written by Monica Hughes
Illustrated by Michael Emmerson

Pat has a go at a jig.

Bev can go on and on.
Bev wins!

3

Red Ted has a go.
He zigs and zags.

Bev revs it up and wins!

6

Sis gets a jug of pop.

Sis tips it and wets Bev's wig!

But it is not Bev.
It is Bad Yaz!